NEW ORLEANS

Days and Nights in the Dreamy City

Locals Share Their Favorite Places

Mary Fitzpatrick and Virginia McCollam

Underwritten through the generosity of the Eugenie and Joseph Jones Family Foundation

Published by the Preservation Resource Center of New Orleans

First published in the United States of America in 2013 by

PRESERVATION RESOURCE CENTER OF NEW ORLEANS
923 Tchoupitoulas St.
New Orleans, Louisiana 70130
504.581.7032
www.prcno.org

© 2013 Preservation Resource Center of New Orleans
Designer: Danielle Del Sol
Sales Manager: Averil Oberhelman, aoberhelman@prcno.org, 504.636.3040

Preservation Resource Center of New Orleans is a registered IRS 501 (c) (3) non-profit organization. Since 1974, the mission of the Preservation Resource Center has been to promote the preservation, restoration and revitalization of New Orleans' historic neighborhoods and architecture.

Printed in China
ISBN 978-0-9773165-2-6

Cover image: Time Descends Over Bacchanal, Bywater © Olivia Moran
Map (opposite): © Stamen Design, under a Creative Commons Attribution (CC BY 3.0) license

South
Lakeview

Gentilly Terrace ↑

Parkview

Esplanade
Ridge

Esplanade Avenue

New Marigny

St. Claude Avenue

Tremé

Faubourg
Marigny

Mid-City

Bywater

Canal Street

Vieux
Carré

Carrollton Avenue

Holy Cross

Central Business
District

Algiers Point

Carrollton

Warehouse
District

Broadmoor

Claiborne Avenue

Central City

Lower Garden
District

Garden District

Uptown

St. Charles Avenue

Irish Channel

Magazine Street

**NEW ORLEANS
HISTORIC NEIGHBORHOODS**

Special thanks to principal photographers Charles E. Leche, Olivia Moran, James Shaw and Mark J. Sindler; to blogmaster Adrienne Tregre (www.neworleansfavorites.com) and to designer Danielle Del Sol.

Mary Fitzpatrick has been editor of Preservation Resource Center's award-winning magazine Preservation in Print since 1995. She is the author of two prior books, *New Orleans: Life in an Epic City* and *New Orleans' Favorite Shotguns* (with Alex Lemann). *Days and Nights in the Dreamy City* completes the trilogy benefiting Preservation Resource Center.

Virginia McCollam has worked in film location management from *Interview with a Vampire* in 1994 to *American Horror Story* in 2013. She is a Peabody Award-winning producer for Spike Lee's *The Huey P. Newton Story* and co-writer of *Careless Love* about jazzman Buddy Bolden.

The Presbytere and St. Louis Cathedral, French Quarter © Olivia Moran

MORNING

Even though MORNING CALL never was located in City Park, the current setting is so perfect that it's become a nostalgia trip for me. They've replicated the neon coffee cup sign outdoors. Inside, the wooden arches with incandescent light bulbs and the tile floor give the whole operation an air of authenticity. We haven't had that spirit here since the original Morning Call fled the jurisdiction during a multi-year renovation of the French Market.

David Marcello, Tulane adjunct professor of law and executive director, The Public Law Center

Morning Call, City Park © Charles E. Leche

CAFÉ DU MONDE. In 1972 I moved to New Orleans, and within the first week I was having a café au lait and beignets. Nearly 40 years later it still ranks as one of my favorite places. No matter how the city changes, Café du Monde remains the same. Arguably one of the best cups of coffee. Sitting there watching New Orleans be New Orleans!

David Spielman, photographer

Café Du Monde, French Quarter © Olivia Moran

Growing up in the country back in South Carolina, the only thing I heard was the neighbor's chickens and it was very irritating. Today, the sweetest sound I hear in the air once Carnival approaches is the practicing of the MARDI GRAS INDIAN TRIBES on Dryades Street in Central City.

Howard Conyers, PhD, engineer

Commanche Lil Chiefs © Christopher Porché West

I love walking my dog along BAYOU ST. JOHN, through FORTIER PARK, and over to FAIR GRINDS off Esplanade Avenue for a coffee and a bacon sweet potato biscuit. The walk is virtuous, the biscuit sinful!

Lydia David, writer, Stegner Fellow Stanford Creative Writing Program

Fair Grinds Coffeehouse, Faubourg St. John, Esplanade Ridge © Olivia Moran

THE ALGIERS FERRY. I might see a freighter pass by in the fog or pelicans dive into the river while I gossip with the other regular commuters or just gaze at the French Quarter skyline with my morning cup of coffee. There's something incredibly romantic about crossing the Mississippi River by boat every day, and I feel so blessed that it's a part of my regular routine.

Angie Green, director, Save Our Cemeteries

View from the Algiers Ferry © Charles E. Leche

Our favorite spot in New Orleans is the RIVIERA ROOF AND OBSERVATION DECK of the Omni Royal Orleans Hotel as it was the site of our 1960s WDSU-television show *Second Cup*. The show opened with a long camera pan of the city skyline ending with a shot of us sitting on the observation deck railing with St. Louis Cathedral in the background and the Vieux Carré at our feet. A similar wonderful view can be seen from the top of the Monteleone Hotel.

Bob and Jan Carr, TV personalities

View from the Monteleone, French Quarter © James Shaw

Whenever I introduce someone to New Orleans I take them to the CAKE CAFÉ in the Marigny for breakfast. We sit at a table on the sidewalk, and they soak up the culture and the architecture of the colorful houses all around us. It's always a splendid start to every visit.

Rebecca O' Malley Gipson, historic house specialist

Spain Street, Faubourg Marigny © Olivia Moran

The corner of CHARTRES AND ESPLANADE AVENUE, where I worked solo on a very significant exterior job for six months and kept a journal. Every day at the same time a beautiful female figure in gorgeous outfits strutted by in a one person parade with horns honking. Finally, I just had to come down off the scaffolding and get a better look at this beauty. She wasn't a she, but still pretty striking. I saw police sting operations. I saw a runaway mule buggy. I saw a mobile pharmacy of illicit drugs operating out of a black car servicing the same guy every single day. What a corner.

Theodore Pierre, brickmason, 4th generation craftsman, Tulane Architecture School graduate

Esplanade and Chartres, Faubourg Marigny by Mary Fitzpatrick

AUDUBON PARK. And not just because it's one of the few Uptown venues where my kids can run free like the banshees they are. Audubon is a visual feast that wonderfully complements the fun house feel of the city with a stately equilibrium. The history of the park is dense — its patriarchal oaks harbor secrets from Buffalo Soldiers to the 1884 World's Fair to rebellious adolescents Robert and Gus in Ellen Gilchrist's aptly titled story collection *In the Land of Dreamy Dreams*, which reads like a glossary to the unseen social currents of the uptown neighborhood that the park anchors. Like the fictional and non-fictional children who run through it, the park is simultaneously elegant and wild in its beauty. An oasis.

Elizabeth Beller, reader for Miramax Films, writer

Audubon Park, Uptown © Olivia Moran

Hansen's for snowballs + Danneel Park + aquarium + Jazz Fest + French Quarter for face painting + Children's Museum + zoo + the insectarium to eat chocolate crickets + McGehee School

Mrs. Steinfeld's second grade class, 2012

Children's Museum, Lafayette Square, CBD
by Mark J. Sindler/Louisiana State Museum

Danneel Park, Uptown by Whitney Brooks

Every Sunday morning, I turn right off of Coliseum on Cadiz to Magazine Street where I enter LA BOULANGERIE, greeted by the warmth of fresh baked bread. I buy two croissants to take home for breakfast and two baguettes to be shared with friends over dinner. By the time I walk home, one half of one of the baguettes is always missing.

Iain S. Baird, author (*Two Storms*)

La Boulangerie, Uptown © Olivia Moran

STILL PERKIN' in the Garden District is unique in a city of many coffee shops. Familiar faces mingle with the ordinary and the famous. Most mornings there are meetings of businessmen, non profit directors, city leaders, fundraisers, writers, real estate agents and friends just easing their way into their day. Celebrities living in the neighborhood drop in unnoticed. During political season, it's a venue that cannot be missed for candidates vying for voters. In short, Still Perkin' is an easy place to meet people or have a private moment. I've been doing it almost every day since Katrina.

Ellis Joubert, master silversmith

The only place I want to be until Brennan's Restaurant reopens is sitting here by the banana trees next to ST. AUGUSTINE CHURCH.

Marion Colbert, powder room attendant at Brennan's

Ms. Colbert, Tremé © Olivia Moran

Satchmo Summer Festival Second Line in front of St. Augustine Church, Tremé © Olivia Moran

I was captured by the Baroque beauty of the interior of ST. ALPHONSUS CHURCH in 2004 and have been writing about historic churches ever since.

Deb Burst, author (*Hallowed Halls of Greater New Orleans*)

St. Alphonsus Altar, Lower Garden District by Deb Burst

When I am on Constance Street approaching Josephine, with ST. MARY'S ASSUMPTION, a German church, on one side and ST. ALPHONSUS, an Irish church, on the other, I think also of the French church, Notre Dame de Bon Secour, which was a block away until the 1920s. I am filled with awe at the thought of so many people of German, Irish and French origin filling these streets on their way to Mass. This streetscape emanates the vitality and rich diversity of New Orleans when it was one of the largest cities in the country.

Patricia Gay, PRC executive director

St. Mary's Assumption and St. Alphonsus, Lower Garden District by Averil Oberhelman

You never know what sort of mysteries you'll come across when you walk down ROSALIE ALLEY in Bywater. While technically a public street, it's really no more than an overgrown dirt road lined with Creole cottages, a relic from New Orleans' Caribbean past. I've seen it all down that dimly lit path: gutterpunk shantytowns, art installations, brightly colored murals, even a real voodoo ceremony with all-white outfits, candles and chanting; the magic of New Orleans manifested.

Brandon Dughman, affordable housing development specialist

A perfect daytime weekend sojourn: When it opens at ten-thirty, pop into Joshua Mann Pailet's A GALLERY FOR FINE PHOTOGRAPHY to see his astonishing collection of everyone from Ansel Adams to Helmut Newton and lots of new discoveries in between (including beautiful work by the actress Jessica Lange). Roughly across the street, there's CRESCENT CITY BOOKS where I always find great old art books and cookbooks. Next, order up a Pimm's Cup, the perfect late morning (and hot weather) refreshment, at the NAPOLEON HOUSE. Once fortified, wander down another couple of blocks to the fabulous movie set that is LUCULLUS to browse their extraordinary culinary antiques and maybe pick up some luxuriously heavy monogrammed napkins or some 19th-century Champagne flutes. Finally, I have a leisurely lunch at one of my favorite restaurants, SYLVAIN. Their bloodies are made from fresh tomato juice, the room is dark and cool and stunning, and everything the talented young chef makes is delicious.

Julia Reed, author (*Queen of the Turtle Derby and Other Southern Phenomena*), contributing editor and writer (*Newsweek, Vogue, Garden and Gun*)

Lucullus, French Quarter by Danielle Del Sol

I used to mask with the Wild Tchoupitoulas Indians when I was a kid. I lived by Bayou St. John so when the Indians came to Mid-City on SUPER SUNDAY it was the biggest day of the year.

John Dawson, musician and New Orleans native

Mardi Gras Indians by Joe Sherman

Super Sunday morning, Orleans Avenue, Mid-City
© James Shaw

Well, another year and another RED DRESS. I borrowed this one from my girlfriend's mom. Is that weird? Probably, but it hardly matters. You're parading around the streets of New Orleans in a dress...with 10,000 other men. You got your gays, straights, body builders, priests, tourists, people who have traveled from all over the country, men of every background and ethnicity. It does have a purpose if you're one of the 14 people who actually runs it. The other 9,986 just want to wear a red dress and drink. Some people are wearing some pretty elaborate stuff. That's why I love the place...it's about the characters.

James Shaw, marketing and graphic arts, blogger (thenoladaily.com)

Red Dress Run, French Quarter © James Shaw

When I was growing up in the 1930s at THE CORNER OF AUDUBON AND GREEN STREETS near Tulane University, the houses were mostly raised cottages with dirt basements housing coal-fired heaters that required us to shovel the coal and clean out the clinkers. The street wasn't paved and my family added cypress curbs and later foundation stones from the demolished Southern Railroad Station on Canal Street. Back then, boys my age made extra money by selling programs at Tulane and Sugar Bowl games. Today the raised cottage basements are finished and often occupied by students, the street is paved, and football has long since moved to the Superdome. I still love that street.

Ambassador John G. Weinmann

Audubon Street at Green, Uptown by Mary Fitzpatrick

The Monday before Mardi Gras, my wife Cynthia and her sisters from Pensacola and my brothers from Baton Rouge gather at our home in Bywater. We go to lunch at THE JOINT for smoked ribs. In the evening we sit around sharing wine and enjoying the music from BACCHANAL filtering into our backyard. We add finishing touches to our costumes for the SOCIETY OF ST. ANNE PARADE and stay up all night reminiscing. At sunrise, we enjoy a quick breakfast with Bloody Marys, then off to the parade starting at Lesseps Street.

Maurice Slaughter, Harley-Davidson distributor

Maurice Slaughter in front of his home, Bywater © Charles E. Leche

After the St. Anne Parade, Marigny by Mark J. Sindler/Louisiana State Museum

Talking to the farmers and vendors at the FARMER'S MARKET and buying what's in season. I carry it all home on the streetcar and then start cooking. In July there are peaches and cantaloupes so I make preserves and pies and agua fresca with what I can't eat raw. My favorite time is spring when I can still get the winter vegetables but the strawberries and blueberries are in.

Matt Newman, financial assistant

Farmer's Market, Warehouse District © Charles E. Leche

The shade of LAFAYETTE SQUARE walking from work to lunch at Herbsaint in the summer.

Rose LeBreton, attorney

Lafayette Square, CBD by Mary Fitzpatrick

Strolling early mornings in the LOWER FRENCH QUARTER when last night's revelers are sleeping it off. The streets are quiet but for occasional clop-clops of mules pulling empty buggies toward Jackson Square, and sunlight pools like molten gold on old tile rooftops. Neighbors walking dogs greet one another. Men in aprons hose down sidewalks in front of bars and shops, delivery trucks unload, and restaurant workers wearing kitchen whites amble toward early shifts. Lemon scents the air. I buy a paper at the corner grocery, head to a nearby coffee shop, and thank my stars I live in this vibrant, enchanting neighborhood.

Carolyn Perry, author (*For Better, For Worse: Patient in the Maelstrom*)

Walking in the FRENCH QUARTER to early mass at St Louis Cathedral, then a Bloody Mary to finish the walk. I love it when they are cleaning the streets.

Edward Bruski, RN
Tulane Hospital

Street sweeper in the French Quarter
by Mary Fitzpatrick

41

SCULPTOR ENRIQUE ALFEREZ worked in an Irish Channel church that still contains decades of his ecstatically passionate and serene work. When we're in that sanctuary/studio, surrounded by so much of his great work, Mimi and I feel the range of Rique's tremendous impact on 20th-century New Orleans public art and public places. We connect from there to the stunning screen over the Charity Hospital entrance, the gorgeous neglected figures in the Four Winds Fountain at Shushan Airport, the surprises all over City Park and the many more places all over the city where Rique captured the best of New Orleans emotions and impulses.

Jack Davis, editor and National Trust for Historic Preservation trustee

Bywater © Robert S. Brantley
Alferez Sculpture at Lakefront Airport © Charles E. Leche

I love to walk in the SLICE OF THE CITY BETWEEN CANAL STREET AND POYDRAS, especially at lunchtime on a weekday — the streets are crowded with businessmen, secretaries, waiters, chefs, judges, lawyers, laborers…. It's the 1930s come alive. The architectural backdrop — all the iconic monuments of the New Orleans skyline — feed the feeling of being in another time. In a tradition that hasn't changed in decades, at noon in the CBD, the rich, the poor and everyone in between rub elbows at the lunch counter.

Savannah Strachan Noble, casting director

CBD lunchtime © Olivia Moran

One of my favorite places in New Orleans that always drives home the old worldness of my hometown is the anteroom of the chapel at the St. Roch cemetery called CAMPO SANTO, which on entering appears to be a crazed menagerie of sorts, with a dankness and smell that recalls the Middle Ages. Artificial legs, leg braces, glass eyes and other symbols of human malady are left as a declaration of St. Roch's healing powers. There is an absolutely archaic quality to the peeling walls, the spare change on the floor, and the patina evident on the plaster and porcelain anatomical parts, which reflects New Orleans decay at its absolute best and feels more like a shrine in Sicily than anything in the new world.

John Stirratt, WILCO bassist

St. Roch Cemetery, New Marigny © Olivia Moran

Votive offerings, St. Roch chapel © James Shaw

Our eldest daughter was young, not yet two. We'd been away from New Orleans for a few months, and driving into town she started to talk, to ask for something. We couldn't understand what she wanted, what she was saying, and she became quite upset and frustrated, which was unusual, she normally had a sunny disposition. Whatever it was, she wanted it in the worst way. We finally figured it out. Lemon ice. She wanted lemon ice from ANGELO BROCATO'S. We did not pass go, we drove straight to Mid-City. Problem solved.

Eric Overmyer, writer, producer (*Tremé, St. Elsewhere, Law & Order, The Wire*)

The FOUNTAIN POOL IN THE COOPER PLAZA, which is the center-piece of the zoo, makes me smile every time I see it. The bronze mama elephant resting on her haunches and spouting water with her calves around her and the yawning hippos in the fountain — it's a happy place no matter your age.

Margo Phelps, Citizens for 1 Greater New Orleans education committee chairman

Miriam Walmsley Cooper Plaza at Audubon Zoo, Uptown by Lisa Langhoff

PARKWAY BAKERY & TAVERN to pick up a po-boy and Barq's root beer, then over to **CITY PARK** to hang out under the oaks. From there I go to the **ZULU SOCIAL AID AND PLEASURE CLUB** on North Broad and Orleans Avenue.

Forrest Ricks, Original Right-Hand Man to Zulu Witch Doctor 2011

Parkway Tavern, Esplanade Ridge © J. Stirling Barrett

Late spring. Second date. Bicycle across town through neighborhoods to AUDUBON PARK. Picnic under a big oak (chicken salad with raspberries, apples and fennel and a bottle of light white wine).

Jim Turner, window restorer and builder

Audubon Park © James Shaw

The sight of seersucker suits in spring.

The smell of sweet olive in season.

The sound of streetcars on Saint Charles,

and the touch of the city's sensuous Catholic soul.

Father Byron Miller, National Shrine of Blessed Francis Xavier Seelos

St. Charles streetcar, Garden District © Olivia Moran

Friday lunch at GALATOIRE'S. Reservations not accepted. Table hopping *de rigeur*. Regulars never miss a Friday, or you might as well live in Houston they say. Jack Gordon held court in the same seat for 50 years. Tradition to the max.

Jackie Derks, advertising

Galatoire's, French Quarter by Jackie Derks

Full of seasonal vegetables, flowers and fruit trees amidst an outdoor classroom and grape covered arbors, the EDIBLE SCHOOLYARD is a beautiful oasis and outdoor laboratory for students, teachers and neighbors. A jewel in the Freret neighborhood, it was developed after Hurricane Katrina, bringing beauty and encouragement to those returning to rebuild.

Cathy Pierson, community leader and gardener

Edible Schoolyard bench, Uptown by Mary Fitzpatrick

FRERET STREET, now lined with imaginative new restaurants, funky cafes, and inviting bars full of music and friendly crowds — anything you could need for a fun time.

Georgia Ainsworth, law student

Freret Street, Uptown by Danielle Del Sol

South Peters at Celeste, looking downriver toward the old MARKET STREET POWER PLANT. I came to love this spot because my mind's eye can see what it was 180 years ago: one of the most bustling and dicey places in town. Here lay the uptown flatboat wharf, where thousands of "upcountry" flatboat crews discharged their goods, scrapped their vessels, and headed into town to raise cane. It's a dirt road now, surrounded by overgrown fields and derelict sheds; even the river shifted away from it. But ringed as it is by the entire metropolis, the seemingly mundane open space comes to feel like the nexus of a great emporium — which, in a way, it once was.

Richard Campanella, geographer, author (*Geographies of New Orleans*),
Tulane School of Architecture

South Peters at Celeste, Lower Garden District by Richard Campanella

Stumbling across the blazing yellow SHRINE OF ST. ANN on Ursulines Avenue for the first time, I was thrown for a loop. It looked as if a spaceship had landed amidst the shotguns in the afternoon heat. The shrine is jarringly incongruent with its Tremé surroundings, an opera set that could have been designed by Gaudi and updated by Dali. And yet I have returned again and again because it is a perfect focal point for contemplation. New Orleans is blessed with unique structures, and this peculiar example, entwined with its own religious and demographic stories, is one of my favorites.

Brad Vogel, attorney, former National Trust for Historic Preservation Fellow

Shrine of St. Ann, Esplanade Ridge © Olivia Moran

OUR LADY OF GUADALUPE. I walk through the grotto, and I look at the wall of thanks until my eyes well up. Then I enter the chapel, say hi to St. Expedite and St. Dymphna, and pray. I am not a praying woman, but I pray there. Always.

Carla Bruni, environmental consultant

Our Lady of Guadalupe, Rampart Street, French Quarter © Olivia Moran

No street in the nation feels, sounds and looks like ST. CHARLES AVENUE, alive with the whir, hum, clang and vibration of the streetcar, enveloped by the canopy of 1,000 stately live oaks, and embraced by the most majestic homes. The green Perley Thomas Series 900 streetcars on St. Charles are the oldest operating street railroad in the United States.

Ted LeClercq, attorney, Preservation Resource Center president

St. Charles Avenue, Uptown © Charles E. Leche

Sitting at the back of **SACRED GRINDS**, overlooking the St. Patrick Cemetery, is a great way to while away an afternoon, contemplating life. Sip a latte or go all the way with an "Undead Elvis," a peanut butter and banana smoothie with chocolate and bacon.

MacKensie Cornelius, archaeologist

Sacred Grinds, Canal Street, Mid-City by MacKensie Cornelius

Whenever I visit my mother and her family, I never call ahead. They're always there. Bouquet in hand, I amble through the familiar old neighborhood of miniature houses in ST. LOUIS CEMETERY NO. 3 on Esplanade Avenue toward the marble steps of the Glaudot tomb. I love the childhood ritual of cleaning out the flower urns, filling the vases from the spigot, and arranging the fresh blooms inside. Then five generations of us hang out reminiscing, and later I might have a glass of wine at nearby Café Degas, which is what they'd do.

James Nolan, poet, fiction writer, essayist, translator, 5th generation New Orleanian

ESPLANADE AVENUE, between the river and Rampart Street, gets my vote as the best six blocks in New Orleans. The magic starts with the neutral ground tended by the residents, who can be seen in early morning dragging garden hoses out to water the city property they regard as an extension of their own. There are live oaks, sycamores, crepe myrtles, sago palms, but no set plan and no head gardener. In fact, the whole endeavor is a squatter's dream. On either side of this urban forest is sublime, eclectic historic architecture with no set back from the sidewalk. Esplanade borders the lower Quarter, still a real neighborhood and the Marigny Triangle, the setting for the city's hippest club and bar scene. It just doesn't get any better than this.

Richard Sexton, photographer and author (*Terra Incognita: Photographs of America's Third Coast*)

Esplanade Avenue bordering French Quarter and Marigny © Richard Sexton

When you cross the threshold of GUY'S PO-BOYS on Magazine Street, you're entering a world where it doesn't matter if you're rich or poor, black or white, young or old, or big or small. You're there to sit down with your fellow New Orleanians at the Formica table of life and behold one of the crown jewels of the Crescent City. A po-boy on Leidenheimer's bread blessed with Crystal hot sauce and cooked with love by Marvin.

"Where y'at?" you ask.

"I'm at Guy's." I smile.

Dave Holt, construction specialist, Neighborhood Housing Services

Guy's, Uptown © Olivia Moran

"Aunt Leah and Uncle Edgar" gave everyone of us kids in the old neighborhood an opportunity. Two requirements: You had to go to school and make good grades in order to work at the restaurant. DOOKY CHASE RESTAURANT will always be my very favorite spot in New Orleans.

Emily Braneon, teacher/librarian

Leah Chase in the kitchen of Dooky Chase's, Tremé by Mark J. Sindler/Louisiana State Museum

When I visit THE FLY, I never fail to see a massive cargo ship up close. Among the few people strolling by, I often stand transfixed. A huge ship moves slowly but efficiently upriver. It's captivating that something so large can actually *move*. And it strikes me as timeless — the reason for New Orleans' existence. Nothing has changed about the use of the river other than the size of the vessels. Two hundred years ago, people stood on the bank of the river, just like me on the Fly, watching commerce move, slowly but efficiently, upriver.

Ramsey Green, real estate developer and consultant

THE FLY is the closest thing to being in the country in terms of quiet and serenity that I know in the city. I sometimes bring my yoga mat...or a bottle of wine and watch the sun set.

Bee Fitzpatrick, retailer and co-owner, Orient Expressed

The Fly, Uptown by Mary Fitzpatrick

Four generations of us have been ordering muffalettas dressed with olive salad and a bottle of Barq's root beer at the CENTRAL GROCERY, so when my dad asked to go there for his 86th birthday it wasn't a surprise.

Keith Jung, pressman

Central Grocery, French Quarter
by Mark J. Sindler/Louisiana State Museum

Uglesich's on Baronne Street was to me the quintessentially "down home" New Orleans food experience — an unpretentious neighborhood joint with the freshest, most authentic fried seafood in town. Now that it's history, I'd have to say that DOMILISE'S has taken the crown: Not only the best fried seafood po-boys, but also their French dip roast beef po-boys are to die for.

Taylor Hackford, director, producer, past president of Directors Guild of America

Patti Domilise making roast beef po-boy, Uptown © Charles E. Leche

From the cold days at Tulane Stadium to the colder days at the MERCEDES-BENZ SUPERDOME, nothing has replaced the joy and agony of a Sunday afternoon with the New Orleans Saints.

John McCollam, attorney

Saints Super Bowl victory parade, Tremé, by Mark J. Sindler/Louisiana State Museum

Every other Sunday, the city yields Poydras Street as it becomes the parade ground for the victorious. Emblazoned with gold and fleur de lis, the throng, 80,000 strong, spills forth from the Superdome. Spirits, both liquid and holy, float among the crowd. For a time, amidst the crisp fall air, there exists in this impermanent company a magical atmosphere of euphoria and fraternity.

Bryan W. Fitzpatrick, investment management consultant

Superdome opening night post Katrina
by Mark J. Sindler/Louisiana State Museum

If it's really hot, I am still a complete child when it comes to having a snoball at HANSEN'S or PLUM STREET SNOBALLS. My Aunt Gray and Aunt Pat love the chocolate with condensed milk on the top. They introduced me to that when I was five years old. My partner Dale and I still love the nectar cream, too.

Hal Williamson,
interior designer

Hansen's, Uptown © Olivia Moran

When I come back in town and need to stock the kitchen, I go straight to LANGENSTEIN'S uptown. It is the only place to buy certain New Orleans foods, unobtainable elsewhere, such as daube glacée and sweet potato soufflé. Invariably I run into someone I last saw at Valencia in 1966. It is amazing how, after all these years, they look exactly the same.

Anne Strachan Eichin, lifelong NOLA-ite

The LOMBARD HOUSE and dooryard garden at the corner of Chartres and Bartholomew in Bywater. Once the seat of a large plantation, it is now an island of rural life in what older New Orleanians call "Downtown." The house appears to have drifted in from the West Indies and features airy rooms and slender Creole columns on its gallery, which looks out on the Mississippi. The neighborhood around it was only recently a safe haven for drug traffickers, but now the sidewalks are filled with runners and baby carriages. The Crescent Park, which runs along the river bank from the Lombard House to the French Quarter, is just across the street.

S. Frederick Starr, author (*Une Belle Maison*), jazzman (Louisiana Repertory Jazz Ensemble), Central Asia specialist

The Lombard House, Bywater, © Robert S. Brantley

I have a peculiar fascination with brown water, because I grew up on that stuff. The PONTCHARTRAIN LAKEFRONT was a part of my everyday life growing up in New Orleans — skipping rocks, fishing, building forts, kick the can, hide and seek, football, keg parties, making out, cross country races. So many significant and inspired things happened there. Now my connection to the place is mostly in my spirit, and occasionally taking a nostalgic walk when I come back to town for a visit. As a kid, I took for granted how lucky I was to grow up a few houses from those magical waters. There were sharks and dolphins in there, garfish and alligators, oil rigs and even dead bodies sometimes, not to mention Al Copeland's cigarette boat. It was like a monster soup for a kid, a place where the wild things really were, and at the time my mind was mostly focused on NEVER going in that thing. But now I respect and value it as a beautiful and primordial place, and it often calls me back. I've decided I want my ashes to go in that brown-ass water, because in more ways than one it feels like the place from whence I came.

Jay Duplass, actor and director (*Safety Not Guaranteed, Jeff Who Lives at Home*)

Lake Pontchartrain © Charles E. Leche

I always wanted to live on the water. Good fortune has brought me to a boathouse on Lake Pontchartrain, on BREAKWATER DRIVE. We look out towards Mandeville on the North Shore, no buildings in sight. The lake could be the Pacific Ocean. Green parrots snack on palm trees in front of our deck. We spy on them through the telescope. Sail boats glide over from the Southern Yacht Club. The sunsets could be in French Polynesia. It is as beautiful as anywhere in Key West, the Hamptons, Bora Bora. I have always wanted to live on the water...now I do.

Stephanie Durant, film location manager, producer, former New Orleans Film Commissioner

Sailboats on Lake Pontchartrain by Mary Fitzpatrick

I love the historic JOSEPH BARTHOLOMEW GOLF COURSE in Pontchartrain Park. A beautiful example of landscape architecture designed by Mr. Bartholomew in the '50s, when African Americans were segregated from even parks and green spaces in New Orleans. As an African American he wasn't allowed to play on the courses he built. But in Pontchartrain Park he created a timeless expanse that survived the flood of 2005 and began a legacy of bucolic excellence. It was from this place a seed was planted that allowed me to enter the world with confidence and vision, like all who grew up in this little piece of heaven called Pontchartrain Park.

Wendell Pierce, actor (*The Wire, Treme*)

OAK STREET because it exudes the NOLA bohemian vibe in a less touristy area. People enjoy the city without making fools of themselves.

LeeAnne Sipe, college administrator

Oak Street, Carrollton
© Charles E. Leche

Po-Boy Festival on Oak Street, Carrollton © James Shaw

About an hour before sunset we like to walk around the corner from our house and down ALLARD BOULEVARD off City Park Avenue in Parkview. The trees form a canopy over the Arts and Crafts houses, and the light is inspiring at that time of day. For a semi-annual neighborhood party, neighbors started stringing white bulbs from one side of the street to the other and when they are lit this might be one of the prettiest blocks in the city.

Rene Guitart, IT guy

Allard Boulevard, Parkview © Rene Guitart

I walked into a bar in the Quarter yesterday (a lot of sentences start like that in New Orleans) looking for an up and coming chef who I was interviewing for a travel story. The place was classic dive with a century old patina and a mixed clientele who, shall we say, were having wake up cocktails. I asked where I could locate said chef and was pointed to the rear to a pop-up kitchen, where, in 70 square feet, po-boys were being re-invented using locally-grown ingredients on fresh bread from Dong Phuong. A hundred year-old bar with gourmet food at the back is the DNA of this town. The past squaring up with progress. The bar is called ERIN ROSE and the restaurant in back, KILLER PO BOYS. Both excellent.

Sara Ruffin Costello, writer, former creative director Domino magazine, co-author of *Domino: The Book of Decorating*

The VERTI MART for a shrimp po-boy with Wow sauce, a bag of Zapp's Crawtators and a cold Barq's root beer. I take it to the levee and sit on the ground, watching the river. After that, I love to costume shop on Decatur Street at Le Garage.

Bryan Block,
Historic District
Landmarks Commission plans examiner
and architect

Verti Mart, French Quarter
© Olivia Moran

My favorite moments in New Orleans are when I'm riding my bike on a street full of colorful shotguns and Creole cottages and, suddenly, there is music — live, local and loaded with brass.

Mary Fitzpatrick, editor (*Preservation in Print*)

Shamarr Allen in Faubourg Marigny by Zoe Geauthreaux

My favorite place is to sit on my HENRIETTE DELILLE STREET stoop in Tremé with my husband Adolph, neighbors, or even just alone. With the beautiful architecture of shotgun houses, Creole cottages and St. Augustine Church in my view and the possibility of a second line parade almost any time, I often think about the lives of people who helped shaped the history and culture of this community, how lucky we are to enjoy the environment today, and how important it is to continue contributing to the legacy.

Naydja Domingue Bynum, property developer

Precisely © Christopher Porché West

FORT JACKSON is my day-ride picnic spot. It's po-boys from Butcher or Guy's, if I'm feeling traditional, and a few beers in a cooler and maybe a good book to kill a couple hours reading on the ramparts, watching the cargo ships navigate their way down toward the river passes. For me, the locale calls for a volume of Civil War history because, yeah, I have that little-boy thing going with what some of the Virginians in the region of my birth used to call the War of Northern Aggression.

David Simon, author (*Homicide: A Year on the Killing Streets*), journalist, writer, producer (*The Wire, Treme*)

Fort Jackson, La. by Alysha Jordan

Strolling on MAGAZINE STREET on a beautiful day...stopping along the way for a meal and just seeing where the day takes us. We inevitably find a new shop. It's best with hours in front of us. When Carroll was in middle school it was great fun for her to be dropped off with friends uptown and walk all the way home. Sometimes I'd get a call to come pick up shopping bags, but for them it was a great feeling of independence.

Katherine and Tony Gelderman, 450 Julia Street/800 Magazine developers

Magazine Street, Garden District © Charles E. Leche

ARCHITECTURAL SALVAGE SOURCES, especially The Bank, Ricca's, Preservation Salvage Store and the Green Project. Strolling through the aisles of such places is a delight because they speak volumes about the culture of a city. Plus, you never know what you may find!

John Stubbs, director of Master of Preservation Studies program of Tulane School of Architecture, author (*Time Honored: A Global View of Architectural Conservation*)

Salvaged goods by Mary Fitzpatrick

One of our favorite things in New Orleans is strolling our neighborhood, the GARDEN DISTRICT, at dusk. The air bears wonderful scents and, whether it's a trick of the lighting at that time of day or voodoo, we always notice something we've never seen before, no matter how many times we've been down the same path.

John Goodman, film and TV actor
(*Argo, Roseanne*)

Garden District, Prytania Street by Mark J. Sindler/Louisiana State Museum

The GARDEN DISTRICT. I love the homes, the fences, the trees. Most of all, I love the eclectic neighbors. Sometimes when I sit on the front porch I see tourists taking photos of the homes, funky kids with purple spiked hair, a musician who plays his saxophone for tips and a limousine filled with heaven only knows who driving down the street. I can see all of these in less time than it takes to sip a glass of wine or cup of tea. It's magical and it's home.

Laura Claverie, journalist

Garden District, First Street © Charles E. Leche

I love the glitter that consumes my house when Muse sisters come over to my "Glitterage" to transform old, uncomfortable high heels into signature throws for our MUSES PARADE. I live on the parade route and I love it. My house is a meeting place for family and friends, and parade days are amazing on Napoleon Avenue. The whole neighborhood celebrates with the marching bands and gorgeous floats.

Virginia Saussy,
Krewe of Muses

A CARNIVAL PARADE ROUTE — from people getting their ice chests and ladders situated to the police trucks leading the parade and then, finally, the floats turning the corner. It's an exhilarating feeling.

Ann Heslin, house renovator

Carnival Day, St. Charles Avenue, Garden District by Mary Fitzpatrick

EVENING

I was elated when I walked into my first NOLA apartment (we moved in sight unseen) in the IRISH CHANNEL. From the soaring ceilings to the colorful paint job to the antique fixtures, a New Orleans home is unlike any other. For the first time in a long time, I loved being at home. Having a front stoop was a complete luxury and became one of my favorite places to spend my time. I have enjoyed hours "stooping it" with a friend and a glass of wine, saying hello to people passing by and meeting neighbors. Being able to stay at home and still interact with people gives you a strong sense of being a part of your neighborhood.

Elena Ricci, photographer and nanny

Magazine Street, Lower Garden District © James Shaw

Irish Channel porch © Olivia Moran

The BEND IN THE LEVEE system in the Lower Ninth Ward next to the Industrial Canal near the steamboat houses that has such a fantastic view of the city.

Tina Freeman, photographer

View of CBD from Holy Cross levee © Olivia Moran

The restaurants. We feel at home when we go to certain restaurants because the owners know their clients. I usually order the same thing. For my birthday a couple years ago, Christy took me to GAUTREAU'S for fois gras, chicken and a banana split. When we miss Italy, we head to ITALIAN BARREL where Chef Samantha's veal porcini is not to be missed. Jim and Mathew at MEAUXBAR could not be more welcoming. During oyster season I take myself for a dozen or two oysters at CASAMENTO'S and hang with Pia, a cook who tries to talk me into something other than Mike's perfectly shucked oysters. She hasn't succeeded yet. Where we feel most at home is at our friend Dickie Brennan's new restaurant TABLEAU. I can't wait to host a dinner in their wine room.

Kia Brown, New Orleans transplant

Meauxbar by Mark J. Sindler/Louisiana State Museum

New restaurants with high expectations. CASA BORREGA on O.C. Haley mixes an ethereal Mexico-meets-New Orleans ambiance with authentic Mexican food, while BOOTY'S in the Bywater — a great first date spot — blends international street food with out-there art displays. MARIZA and MAUREPAS, also new in the Bywater, are consistently packed on Friday nights with an uptown/downtown mix of Orleanians. Pop-up cocktail and dinner events around the city — and the growing food truck scene — keep it fresh.

Danielle Del Sol, writer and editor
(*Preservation in Print*)

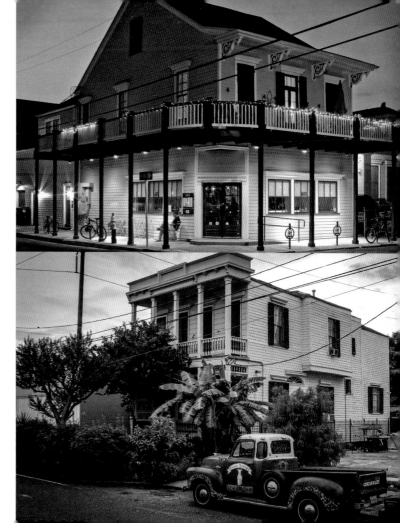

Booty's, Bywater © Olivia Moran

Casa Borrega, Central City © James Shaw

One of my favorite things to do in New Orleans is to sit on the swings in front of the PORT AUTHORITY building. From these swings you can see the underbelly of the Crescent City Connection and watch the ships pass on the Mississippi.

Suzy Mason, executive director, Louisiana GreenCorps

1350 Port of New Orleans Place © Olivia Moran

My favorite memory of the PRYTANIA THEATER was when the streetcars passed in both directions in front of the theater. Back then, the movie sound was on records and so when you were inside and the streetcars went by, well, the building would shake and the needle would jump to the next groove, which put the picture out of sync with the sound. Today, I like greeting visitors and taking tickets at the door of the theater, and I like going on stage and talking about the movies before they start and sharing my remembrances.

Rene Brunet, Prytania Theater owner

The Prytania, Uptown © Olivia Moran

Rene Brunet in front of Prytania courtesy Robert Brunet

What I love about New Orleans is ephemeral — the smell of rain in summer, sweet olive in the dead of winter, jasmine at night and the frying shrimp from the take-out po-boys wafting down from the 24-hour deli on the corner of my block of Ursuline Street in the Quarter. And then the architecture, reminding me always that I live in a privileged continuum where beauty has always had the spotlight — and the citizens, music and food, tempered by its effects. As a photographer, New Orleans is indispensable as an inspiration. Trying to describe it, as the great Brazilian writer Clarice Lispector said, is like "trying to photograph perfume."

Josephine Sacabo, photographer

Peristyle, City Park © Josephine Sacabo

I am forever grateful to LE PETIT THEATRE for giving me my theatrical start. I am pleased to have served more recently on the board of directors, which masterminded the saving of our precious jewel box theatre by selling parts of the complex to The Dickie Brennan Group. Now with the theatre intact and fully renovated, one can dine or sip a cocktail at the new world-class restaurant Tableau and marvel at the most breathtaking views of the French Quarter. It's a perfect example of how old and new work side by side in our magical…and theatrical city.

Bryan Batt, stage, TV (*Mad Men*) and film actor, designer and author (*She Ain't Heavy, She's My Mother*)

Le Petit Theatre, French Quarter, before building conversion
© Charles E. Leche

Thirty-four years ago while visiting New Orleans, I was lured into the NAPOLEON HOUSE by its warmly lit ambience and aura of history. It was on that night, while I sipped a Pimm's Cup at a table inlaid with a chessboard, that I decided to move to New Orleans. Two months later I was living in Carrollton and I'm still here, and I still love the Napoleon House.

Celeste Berteau writer and veterinary clinic receptionist

Napoleon House, French Quarter © J. Stirling Barrett

It happens this way. I'm driving along some oak-shrouded street in Mid-City and I hit BAYOU ST. JOHN from the back end. It's always a shock, even when I'm not lost. The world opens. I'm stunned by the sunlight, staggered by the panorama. The bayou shimmers. Ducks glide on the water. A car creeps down Moss Street. On either side of the bayou lies an entire history, written in architecture. West Indies plantations sit cheek by jowl with shotgun houses and Greek Revival cottages. There are Arts and Crafts bungalows, brick ramblers, an occasional modern façade. I'd know where I was even if I'd never set foot in Louisiana, if I'd been blindfolded and set loose here. New Orleans. Home.

John D. Gray, writer

Views of Bayou St. John, Esplanade Ridge © James Shaw

The MAGNOLIA BRIDGE across Bayou St. John, a beautiful foot bridge for lingering at sunrise or sunset.

Anne Morse, preservationist

When I want to escape population density and have a strong friend with me, I love portaging my canoe from BAYOU ST. JOHN into City Park and paddling underneath all the footbridges and through the sculpture garden, then parking behind Morning Call and getting some beignets. I also love playing music in the evening with friends at the bridge, underneath the section with the Christmas lights.

Kim Vu-Dinh, compliance consultant

Magnolia Bridge, Bayou St. John, Esplanade Ridge © Charles E. Leche

In the summer, considering temperature and proximity, a tour of the museums and galleries of the WAREHOUSE DISTRICT followed by a cold cocktail (complete with plastic swordfish) at Lucy's.

Sonny Shields, attorney

Lucy's Retired Surfer's Bar, Warehouse District © Charles E. Leche

We probably go 50 times a year to the OGDEN MUSEUM OF SOUTHERN ART on Thursday night. We go for the art, the music, the food and the people. They've had performances by Trombone Shorty, Henry Butler, Little Freddie King, Dave Pirner from Soul Asylum, and so many more. The food by Miss Linda, the Yakamein Lady, is great — of course, you've had yakamein, that spicy mix of meat, eggs, green onions and noodles with soy sauce. It's called "Old Sober" because it helps get rid of hangovers. New Orleanians love it!

Sara Moore, Rebuilding Together community outreach
Craig Moore, civil engineer

St. Claude Avenue, and the Marigny, Bywater, St. Roch and Tremé neighborhoods, on the SECOND SATURDAY of every month when the artist cooperatives and art galleries have their openings. The streets and neighborhoods come alive.

Charles Whited, Jr., attorney

St. Claude art opening night, New Marigny © Olivia Moran

My New Orleans divides into two essential categories: familiar places I love and long dreamy explorations, often via Vespa, during which I encounter and re-encounter certain landscapes and images. One late-summer evening, I happened along a stretch of BURGUNDY NEAR ALVAR STREET, a block whose only distinguishing landmark is the library, an Art Deco structure of pale limestone, distinctly urban and unexpected. I later discovered it was where Lee Harvey Oswald went often as a kid, where he got an education of sorts. This adds a layer of spookiness. There's a large house in that block too, lovely in its dilapidation, painted a blue somewhere between navy and royal and, on that day, tattooed with a red graffiti heart. Out front sat a huge willow and a string of vintage cars that straddled the line between collector's items and junk. It was dusk. I fell in love. The block became a touchstone of future rambles, a recurring dream. None of it has any permanence, save perhaps the library and the huge willow. Last time I went by the heart was gone. But the soul of the street remains.

Thomas Beller, author (*The Sleep-Over Artist*), editor (*How To Be a Man: Essays*)

Alvar Street Branch, Bywater by Mary Fitzpatrick

I've been around JULIA STREET through all the changes. In 1968 or '69, the Camp Inn was in the Guinness Book of Records because they served 1,125,000 bottles of wine. In 1975 I was here when "Hard Times" was filmed, and the star Charles Bronson got his hair cut at Freddie's Barber Shop in this weird 1920s look when they had bare-knuckle fights. I've lived around here in hotels, apartments and a parking lot on St. Charles. I like to go to Martha's to eat (Louisiana Products), and when I was a mechanic I stored my tools at Tony's (New Orleans Plating & Polishing.) I'm friends with the art gallery owners, most everyone knows me.

M.C. Brown, ex-Marine, mechanic and drifter (deceased 2013)

M.C. on Julia Row, Lafayette Square District, CBD
courtesy Jean Bragg Gallery

Gallery opening night on Julia Row © Charles E. Leche

EUCLID RECORDS. Guarded by the spirit of Ernie K-Doe, this pink palace in the Bywater is a primary reason I decided to move to the neighborhood. Its low key atmosphere and expertly curated collection of new and old music proves the better tonic again and again. Save your money at the bar and head down to the corner of Chartres and Desire.

Jay Steele,
music promoter

Euclid Records, Bywater © Olivia Moran

I walked by the old Holy Trinity in Marigny and beautiful music was wafting through the air. In the derelict empty church a man was playing the piano. There was a sofa so I sat and just listened. Turns out he owns the church and has transformed it into a private performance space called the MARIGNY OPERA HOUSE.

Mary Morrow, designer, producer, mom

Marigny Opera House, Faubourg Marigny © Olivia Moran

New Orleans restaurants when the owners, waiters and maitre d's make patrons feel so welcome. COMMANDER'S PALACE with Lally or Ti, RALPH'S ON THE PARK when Kathryn Brennan is there, PATOIS with Pierre, ANTOINE'S when Jimmy Campara is in charge of the table, and ANNUNCIATION when Richard Williams is running the show (and show it is).

Laura Singletary, attorney

Commander's Palace, Garden District by Evan Gabriel

Richard Williams at Annunciation, Warehouse District by Mary Fitzpatrick

Ralph's on the Park, Parkview © Charles E. Leche

I would start out with a drive to New Orleans East and visit the incredible Vietnamese bakery, DONG PHUONG, for a freshly made banh mi/Vietnamese po-boy. Then I would drift to the French Quarter, to the upstairs at ARNAUD'S restaurant to visit their "Mardi Gras Museum," which is not only air-conditioned, but also houses over two dozen Mardi Gras court costumes of Germaine Cazenave Wells, the daughter of Count Arnaud. After exposure to the overwhelming bevy of encrusted jewels, there's only one thing left to do: meander downstairs and wash that information down with a perfect Ramos Gin Fizz at the French 75 bar. Once the sun begins to edge off of the city and creep towards Texas, I'd take a walk through CITY PARK and end the day in Bywater with a slice of pizza at PIZZA DELICIOUS.

Helen Hollyman, food editor, VICE magazine

Mixologist Chris Hannah at French 75 bar, French Quarter © Charles E. Leche

TIPITINA'S when my son is playing guitar for the Stooges Brass Band or with his own band Minutehead. I never thought I would be frequenting Tipitina's at this point, but it has made me really appreciate the great music of New Orleans.

Kathy Slater, table designer

Tipitina's, Uptown © Olivia Moran

I go to TRINITY ARTIST SERIES on Sunday nights to be surprised and delighted at the quality, depth and variety of New Orleans' musical talent. From symphony artists to Dancing-Man504 to very young horn students taking a spontaneous lesson from Delfeayo Marsalis, Manon and Albinas have created magical programs that make me feel lucky to be in this place and time.

Ann D. Stevens, IT consultant

Trinity Church Artist Series, Lower Garden District
by Manon Prizgintas

The huge front porch of **THE COLUMNS HOTEL**, sipping mimosas with friends. The Columns is a masterpiece, built in the late 1800s and beautifully restored. Its location on the St. Charles streetcar line makes it the perfect place to reflect on how much I love New Orleans.

Kim Bookless, writer and editor

Columns Hotel on St. Charles Avenue, Uptown © Olivia Moran

COTÉ SUD restaurant on Maple Street in Carrollton — small and intimate with candlelight, the best mussels in town and excellent wines.

Alma Slatten, civic leader

Coté Sud, Maple Street, Carrollton
© Charles E. Leche

NIGHT

THE ST. LOUIS CATHEDRAL.
Situated in the center of the old city, it
stands as a reminder of God's presence
and providence through centuries of routine, ruin and rebirth.

Jay Adkins, 4th generation Baptist pastor

Night in the Marigny © James Shaw

St. Louis Cathedral, French Quarter © Charles E. Leche

A picnic at night on the ALGIERS POINT LEVEE. We pack up a wicker basket with Wedgwood china and a wonderful spread from Tout Suite Café, which is just blocks away. We lay out two linen cloths and use a candlelight storm lantern to enjoy the most remarkable view of the city there is. The light from the bridge, the city and the moon shimmer on the river, disturbed only by passing paddle wheelers and ships. You see the city in its entirety, both past and present, from the historic cathedral and the French Quarter to the modern skyline of downtown.

Marco St. John, contractor/artist
Anais St. John, jazz vocalist

July 4th fireworks viewed from Algiers Point © James Shaw

In the early evening we love to sit on our balcony at the end of Walnut Street uptown watching boats of all sizes move up and down THE RIVER: a constant reminder of how New Orleans came to be and how it has thrived for nearly three centuries.

Dr. Stephen Hales, pediatrician

One of my favorite things to do, on a sweltering evening, is to arm myself with a cool libation and to walk with friends over to FRENCHMEN STREET. I like to stand in the street and hear the music coming out of the doors. I like to walk up and down and sample a Marsalis here, a horn stomper there, some reggae boys down at the end of the block, oh and who the hell is the new chanteuse at the Spotted Cat and why is she great in a way that singers are never great in any other city but New Orleans?

Mark Childress, novelist
(*Crazy in Alabama*)

Frenchmen Street, Faubourg Marigny © Charles E. Leche

Spotted Cat, Faubourg Marigny © Olivia Moran

I love heading out in the summer with as little clothing as one can get away with to the courtyard at BACCHANAL in Bywater to listen to a gypsy jazz band, sip some wine and eat some good food around a big table, surrounded by longtime friends and people just met by virtue of the seating arrangement, with the breeze blowing in off the river, the Christmas lights twinkling around me and the smell of jasmine scenting the air.

Emilie Bahr, urban planner

Bacchanal, Bywater © Olivia Moran

New Orleans is the one place in this country where I find I can be myself. Doesn't matter what age you are or what you are wearing. At work, on set, I'd often just wear a pair of Levis and a T-shirt and then go out to DBA, Snug Harbor or the Spotted Cat on Frenchmen Street to hear some music after we wrapped. No one stopped me at the door because of a dress code, and no one cared that I had gray in my hair. I was always welcome wherever. Folks talked to me, whether I was in line at Rouse's, riding the ferry across the mighty Mississippi, or sitting at the bar of a restaurant having dinner by myself. So it's one thing that I miss when I am away from New Orleans. It's the people. In New Orleans, I never feel like I am alone.

George Pelecanos, novelist (*The Night Gardener*), producer, scriptwriter

Snug Harbor, Frenchmen Street, Faubourg Marigny © Charles E. Leche

Pelecanos (pictured left) in DBA, Marigny by Virginia McCollam

My favorite place on Monday night is the HI HO LOUNGE on St. Claude Avenue. Why Monday? Because that's when the Bluegrass Pickin' Party happens. Anyone is welcome to bring instruments and sit down to play with a group of friends and strangers alike. No tips, no fame, just a love of bluegrass. And if that isn't enough, they sell red beans and rice from the kitchen at $2.00 a bowl.

Patrick Raber, graduate student
LSU Health Sciences Center

Sunday night at KAJUN'S PUB on St. Claude Avenue when JD and the Jammers are performing. It is so unassuming, well, one could even call it a "dive," but the entertainment is so to my liking. Genuine Blues. JD himself is very entertaining just to watch. Last time I was there they wowed me with an improv performance together with a guest of the bar, Mr. Freddie King. They rendered "House of the Rising Sun" — dreamy and delightful.

Chiara Jacobson, Italian teacher

Kajun's Pub on St. Claude Avenue, New Marigny © Olivia Moran

There is a truly unique little place on the more neighborhood side of Oak Street called (and I'm not kidding here) "SNAKE AND JAKE'S CHRISTMAS LOUNGE CLUB." Now, there are many defining characteristics of this great, hidden gem of a dive bar uptown. Late night tamales? Check. The opportunity to celebrate Christmas every night of the year? Check. Open at 7am? Yep. Check. There are even bumper stickers that proudly proclaim "eaux yeah" if one is so inclined. But the greatest thing about this place is that it sits right in the middle of a cozy neighborhood street, and you can stroll in anytime and usually find someone telling a very odd, potentially disturbing personal story. And you get to say "Merry Christmas" right back without a hint of irony, and then buy that person an incredibly well-priced beer.

Mark Duplass, actor and director (*Zero Dark Thirty, Safety Not Guaranteed, Jeff Who Lives at Home*)

Snake and Jake's, Carrollton © Julia Allen

The MAPLE LEAF BAR on Oak Street in Carrollton, where you can smell, feel and hear the funk!

Anne Balser Legge, animation colorist, *The Simpsons*

Maple Leaf on Oak Street, Carrollton
© Charles E. Leche

The truck parked in front of JACQUES IMO'S on Oak Street in Carrollton looks like a piece of junk. I'm not even sure if it runs. But there is no more magical feeling than perching in its bed on a hot summer evening, keeping the sweat at bay with an icy watermelon mojito and indulging in a greasy, thick slice of alligator cheesecake. If you're lucky and a brass band happens along, this is the perfect place to watch the crowds draw around, to feel like the center of attention without ever being noticed — which is, of course, one of the great joys of life in New Orleans.

Sarina Mohan, urban planner and educator

Jacques Imo's on Oak Street, Carrollton © Olivia Moran

In New Orleans the air is heavy. You have the sense that if you stand in one place long enough the ground might shift beneath your feet and all that New Orleans is might be sunk back into the swamp. It's hot. So you push into a dark bar room, cooled to freezing by an old Friedrich's wall unit, terra-cotta chip floor, a juke box filling the air with soul — wherever I am, I remember these places, like BOCAT'S LOUNGE on Orleans Avenue, VAUGHAN'S down in the Bywater or BULLET'S on A.P. Tureaud — Kermit Ruffin's horn blowing, ribs and sausage smoking on the grill — Katrina didn't take us, I don't think anything will.

Virginia McCollam, film location manager